Learn JAPANESE Through Fairy Tales

GOLDILOCKS and the 3 BEARS

Book Design & Production: Slangman Kids *(a division of Slangman Inc. and Slangman Publishing)*

Copy Editor: Julie Bobrick
Illustrated by: "Migs!" Sandoval
Translator: Mariko Bird

Published by: Slangman Kids *(a division of Slangman Inc. and Slangman Publishing)* 12206 Hillslope Street, Studio City, CA 91604 •USA • Toll Free Telephone from USA: 1-877-SLANGMAN (1-877-752-6462) • From outside the USA: 1-818-SLANGMAN (1-818-752-6462) • Worldwide Fax 1-413-647-1589 • Email: info@slangman.com • Website: www.slangman.com

"Migs!" Sandoval
✷ our illustrator ✷

Miguel *"Migs!"* Sandoval has been drawing cartoons since the age of 6 and has worked on numerous national commercials and movies as a sculptor, model builder, and illustrator. He was born in Los Angeles and was raised in a bilingual household, speaking English and Spanish. He currently lives in San Francisco where he is working on his new comic book series!

ISBN10: 1891888-846
ISBN13: 978189888-847
Printed in the U.S.A.

10 9 8 7 6 5 4 3 2 1

Order Form

Preview chapters & shop online!
www.slangman.com

SHIP TO: _____

_____

_____

Contact/Phone/Email: _____

SHIPPING

Domestic Orders

SURFACE MAIL
(Delivery time 5-7 business days).
Add $5 shipping/handling for the first item, $1.50 for each additional item.

RUSH SERVICE
Available at extra charge. Contact us for details.

International Orders

SURFACE MAIL
(Delivery time 6-8 weeks).
Add $6 shipping/handling for the first item, $2 for each additional item. Note that shipping to some countries may be more expensive. Contact us for details.

AIRMAIL (approx. 3-5 business days)
Available at extra charge. Contact us for details.

Method of Payment (Check one):

☐ Personal Check or Money Order
(Must be in U.S. funds and drawn on a U.S. bank.)

☐ VISA ☐ Master Card ☐ Discover ☐ American Express ☐ JCB

☐☐☐☐ ☐☐☐☐ ☐☐☐☐ ☐☐☐☐

Credit Card Number

_____   ☐☐ ☐☐
Signature   Expiration Date

QTY	ISBN-13	TITLE	PRICE	LEVEL	TOTAL COST
English to CHINESE (Mandarin)					
	9781891888-793	Cinderella	$14.95	1	
	9781891888-854	Goldilocks	$14.95	2	
	9781891888-915	Beauty and the Beast	$14.95	3	
English to FRENCH					
	9781891888-755	Cinderella	$14.95	1	
	9781891888-816	Goldilocks	$14.95	2	
	9781891888-878	Beauty and the Beast	$14.95	3	
English to GERMAN					
	9781891888-762	Cinderella	$14.95	1	
	9781891888-830	Goldilocks	$14.95	2	
	9781891888-885	Beauty and the Beast	$14.95	3	
English to HEBREW					
	9781891888-922	Cinderella	$14.95	1	
	9781891888-939	Goldilocks	$14.95	2	
	9781891888-946	Beauty and the Beast	$14.95	3	
English to ITALIAN					
	9781891888-779	Cinderella	$14.95	1	
	9781891888-823	Goldilocks	$14.95	2	
	9781891888-892	Beauty and the Beast	$14.95	3	
English to JAPANESE					
	9781891888-786	Cinderella	$14.95	1	
	9781891888-847	Goldilocks	$14.95	2	
	9781891888-908	Beauty and the Beast	$14.95	3	
English to SPANISH					
	9781891888-748	Cinderella	$14.95	1	
	9781891888-809	Goldilocks	$14.95	2	
	9781891888-861	Beauty and the Beast	$14.95	3	
Japanese to ENGLISH　絵本で えいご を学ぼう					
	9781891888-038	Cinderella	$14.95	1	
	9781891888-045	Goldilocks	$14.95	2	
	9781891888-052	Beauty and the Beast	$14.95	3	
Korean to ENGLISH　동화를 통한 ENGLISH 배우기					
	978189188	Cinderella			
	97818918				
	97818918				
Spanish to EN					
	97818918				
	97818918				
	97818918				

Sales Tax (

Prices subject to change

SLANGMAN KIDS

(a division of Slangman Publishing)

** TO PLACE AN ORDER – CALL, FAX, OR EMAIL
Phone: 1-818-752-6462 • Fax: 1-413-647-1589
Email: info@slangman.com • Web: www.slangman.com
12206 Hillslope Street • Studio City, CA 91604

(FORM 071606

Dedication

The entire "Foreign Language Through Fairy Tales" series is dedicated to all the children of the world.

It is through their understanding, appreciation, and celebration of our differences that the world will become a better and safer place for us all.

One thing to remember...

The words in **green italics** throughout this fairy tale are words you've already learned in the previous level! Do you still remember what they mean?

1

kuma くま

kuma no papa くまのパパ

kuma no mama くまのママ

Once upon a time, there was a [bear] family that lived in a *yeh* in the forest – a [papa bear] who was extremely *okeena*, a very *kawa-ee* [mama bear], and their pride and joy, a cute

2

baby bear. The **kuma no akachan** was very little. The **cheesana kuma no akachan** was also very *hansamna* like the *okeena* **kuma no papa**. They were proud of their **kuma** family.

**kuma
no akachan**
くまのあかちゃん

cheesana
ちいさな

3

One day, the **kuma no mama** prepared some soup for the **kuma no papa** and the **cheesana kuma no akachan**, but it was too hot. While it cooled off, the **kuma** family went for a stroll.

Meanwhile in a town nearby, there lived an *onanoko*, who was very *kawa-ee*, named Goldilocks. She was very *kanashee* because she never had anything fun to do.

5

She thought for a ***chotto-no-aida*** and
decided to take a **sanpo** in the forest.
Very soon, she came upon a **yeh** and
knocked on the door but no one was there.

doa
ドア

So she opened the **doa**, put one *ashi*
inside the *yeh*, and said "Hello? Is anyone
home?" She was very ⌈tired⌉ after her
long **sanpo** and since no one answered,

ts'kareta
つかれた

7

teh-buru
テーブル

keetcheen
キッチン

she walked slowly inside the **yeh**. She looked around the **yeh** and was very **shiawaseh** to see a an **okeena** table in the kitchen with bowls of food on it!

8

She quickly approached the *okeena*

teh-buru in the **keetcheen** and was super

extra *shiawaseh* because there on the

teh-buru in the **keetcheen** was a bowl —

bo'o-ru
ボウル

9

eechee ←
いち

nee ←
に

san ←
さん

but not just one **bo'oru**. There were one, two, three of them! **Eechee**, **nee**, **san** sitting on the *okeena* **teh-buru** in the **keetcheen**. She took a taste from the *okeena* **bo'oru** that belonged to

the **kuma no papa** and said, "This is too hot!" ──► **atsui**
あつい

Then she took a taste from the **bo'oru** that

belonged to the **kuma no mama** and said,

"This is too cold!" Then she took a taste from ──► **ts'metai**
つめたい

11

the **cheesana bo'oru** of the **cheesana kuma no akachan** and said, "Ah. This one isn't too **atsui**. It isn't too **ts'metai**. It's just right!" The **bo'oru** was very **cheesana** and she ate

everything in it. Well, now she was even more
ts'kareta than ever after eating so much.
So, she decided to rest. In the living room,
she saw a chair...but not just one **eesu**.

eesu
いす

13

There were **eechee**, **nee**, **san** of them!
Eechee, **nee**, **san**! So, she sat down in
the *okeena* **eesu** of the **kuma no papa**
and said, "Oh! This **eesu** is too [hard]!"

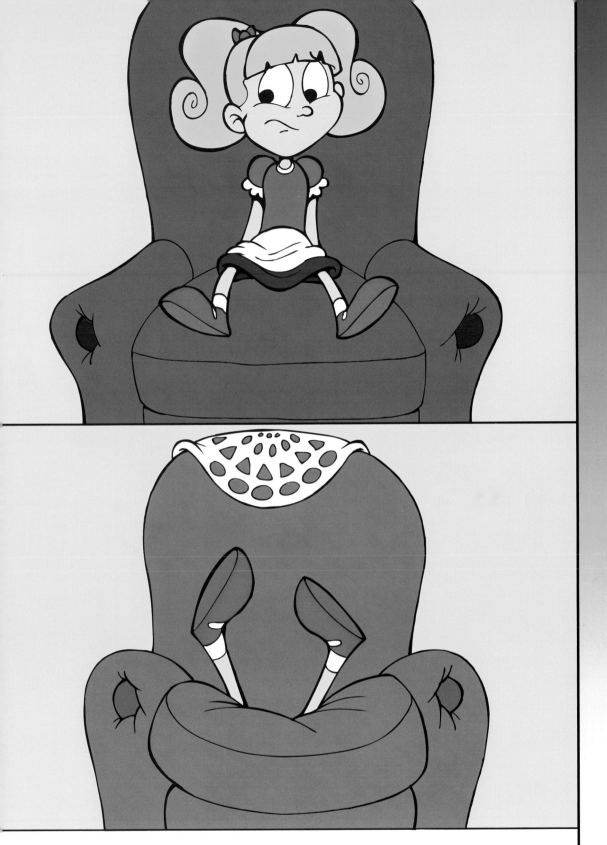

So, she sat in the **eesu** of the **kuma no mama** and said, "Oh! This **eesu** is too soft!"
Then she sat in the **cheesana eesu** of the **cheesana kuma no akachan** and said,

→ **yawarakai**
やわらかい

"Ah. This **cheesana eesu** isn't too **katai**. It isn't too **yawarakai**. It's just right!" But just as she got comfortable... *Crack!* The **eesu** broke and completely fell apart!

Still **ts'kareta**, she decided to look for the bedroom to take a nap. In front of her, she saw a [bed]... but not just one **beddo**. There were **eechee**, **nee**, **san** of them!

beddo
ベッド

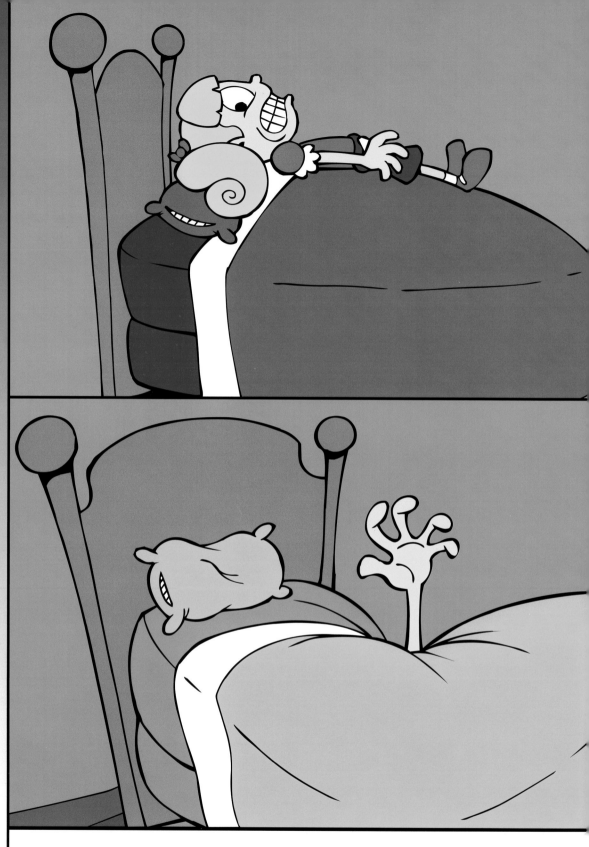

Eechee, **nee**, **san**! So, she tried the *okeena* **beddo** of the **kuma no papa**, but it was too **katai**. Then she tried the **beddo** of the **kumo no mama**, but it was too **yawarakai**. Finally,

she tried the **beddo** of the **cheesana kuma no akachan** and said, "Ah. This **beddo** isn't too **katai**. It isn't too **yawarakai**. It's just right!" And she fell asleep. At that very *chotto-no-aida*, the **kuma** family returned from their **sanpo**. As they walked in the **keecheen**, the *okeena* **kuma no papa** noticed something strange. "Someone's been eating my soup!" growled the *okeena*

kuma no papa. "And someone's been eating my soup!" said the **kuma no mama**. "And someone's been eating MY soup and ate it all up!" cried the **cheesana kuma no akachan**.

"Look!" said the *okeena* **kuma no papa**.

"Someone's been sitting in my **eesu**!"

"And someone's been sitting in my **eesu**, as well!" said the **kuma no mama**.

"And someone's been sitting in my **eesu** and broke it into pieces!" cried the **cheesana kuma no akachan**. Then, the **kuma no papa**, the **kuma no mama**, and the **cheesana**

kuma no akachan heard snoring coming
from the bedroom, so they went in to look.
"Someone's been sleeping in my **beddo**!" said the
okeena kuma no papa. "And someone's been

sleeping in my **beddo**," said the **kuma no mama**. "And someone's been sleeping in my **cheesana beddo** and there she is!" shouted the **cheesana kuma no akachan**.

Just then, Goldilocks woke up and was very surprised to see the **kuma** family! The **kuma** family thought the **cheesana** *onanoko* was very *eejeewaru* to use their *yeh*

without permission! "Oh, *arigato!*" Goldilocks
said to the **kuma no papa**. "*Arigato* for letting
me eat food from your **bo'oru**, sit in your **eesu**,
and lie in your **beddo**. *Arigato!*" she said again,

expecting the **kuma** family to say, "*doita-shimashteh!*" but they were angry that she caused so much trouble in their **yeh** and the **kuma** family growled at her. So, she slowly

stood up on the **cheesana beddo** of the **cheesana kuma no akachan**, and nervously said, "Well, *arigato* for having me and... *sayonara!*" And with that, Goldilocks

jumped off the **cheesana beddo**, and dashed out the front **doa**, running as fast as each *ashi* could move. Needless to say, she never returned to visit the **yeh** of the **kuma** family again.